SUPER BOWL CHAMPIONS
MIAMI DOLPHINS

QUARTERBACK
RYAN TANNEHILL

SUPER BOWL CHAMPIONS

MIAMI DOLPHINS

AARON FRISCH

CREATIVE PAPERBACKS

Published by Creative Paperbacks
P.O. Box 227, Mankato, Minnesota 56002
Creative Paperbacks is an imprint of The Creative Company
www.thecreativecompany.us

Design and production by Blue Design
Art direction by Rita Marshall
Printed in the United States of America

Photographs by Getty Images (Atlantide Phototravel,
Joel Auerbach, Doug Benc, Bruce Bennett Studios, Sam
Greenwood, Norm Hall, Rod Hanna/NFL, Bob Levey,
Takashi Makita/NFL, NFL Photos, Darryl Norenberg/NFL,
JC Ridley/NFL, George Rose, Marc Serota, RHONA WISE/
AFP)

Library of Congress Cataloging-in-Publication Data
Frisch, Aaron.
Miami Dolphins / Aaron Frisch.
p. cm. — (Super bowl champions)
Includes index.
Summary: An elementary look at the Miami Dolphins
professional football team, including its formation in 1966,
most memorable players, Super Bowl championships, and
stars of today.
ISBN 978-1-60818-379-1 (hardcover)
ISBN 978-0-89812-958-8 (pbk)
1. Miami Dolphins (Football team)—History—Juvenile
literature. I. Title.

GV956.M47F75 2014
796.332'6409759381—dc23   2013010637

First Edition
9 8 7 6 5 4 3 2 1

DEFENSIVE TACKLE
MANNY FERNANDEZ

JASON TAYLOR / 1997–2007, 2009, 2011
Jason was a fast defensive end who won an award in 2006 as the NFL's best defensive player.

TABLE OF CONTENTS

WIDE RECEIVER
PAUL WARFIELD

SOUND IT OUT
BUONICONTI:
bwah-nih-KAHN-tee

GRIDIRON DOLPHINS

Many dolphins swim in the ocean near Miami, Florida. But people can also see Dolphins on land in Miami—as the National Football League's (NFL) Dolphins team!

8

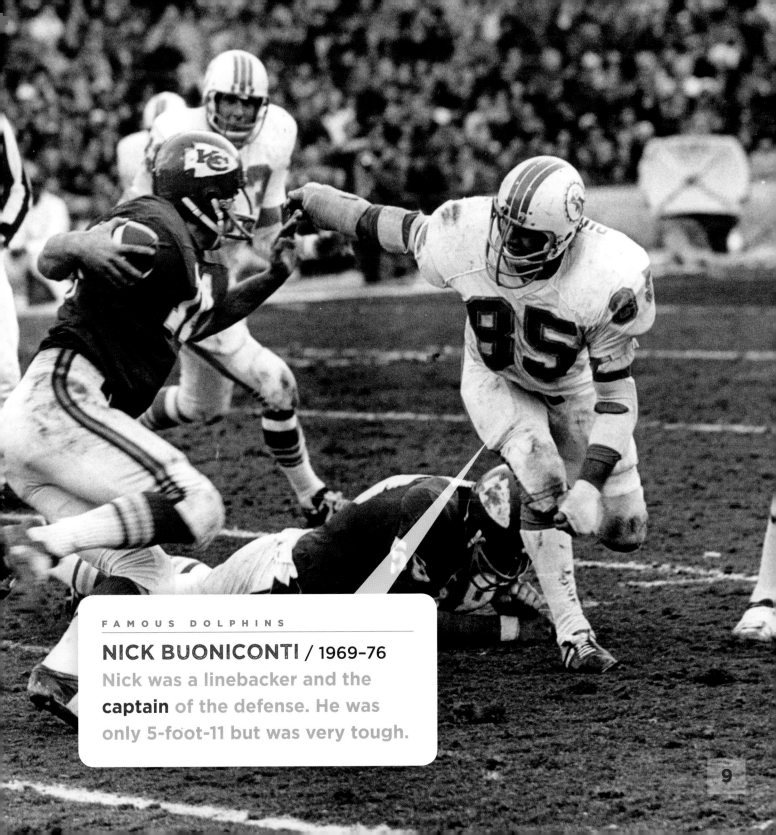

NICK BUONICONTI / 1969–76

Nick was a linebacker and the **captain** of the defense. He was only 5-foot-11 but was very tough.

WELCOME TO MIAMI

Miami has many beaches and palm trees. It is very warm for almost the whole year. Many people like to take vacations or go fishing there.

LARRY CSONKA

1968–74, 1979

Larry was a powerful running back who liked to run over opponents. Fans called him "Zonk."

SOUND IT OUT

CSONKA: *ZONG-kuh*

THE PERFECT TEAM

The Miami Dolphins are famous for being the only NFL team in history not to lose a game in a season. In 1972, they won all 16 of their games. Miami was the perfect team!

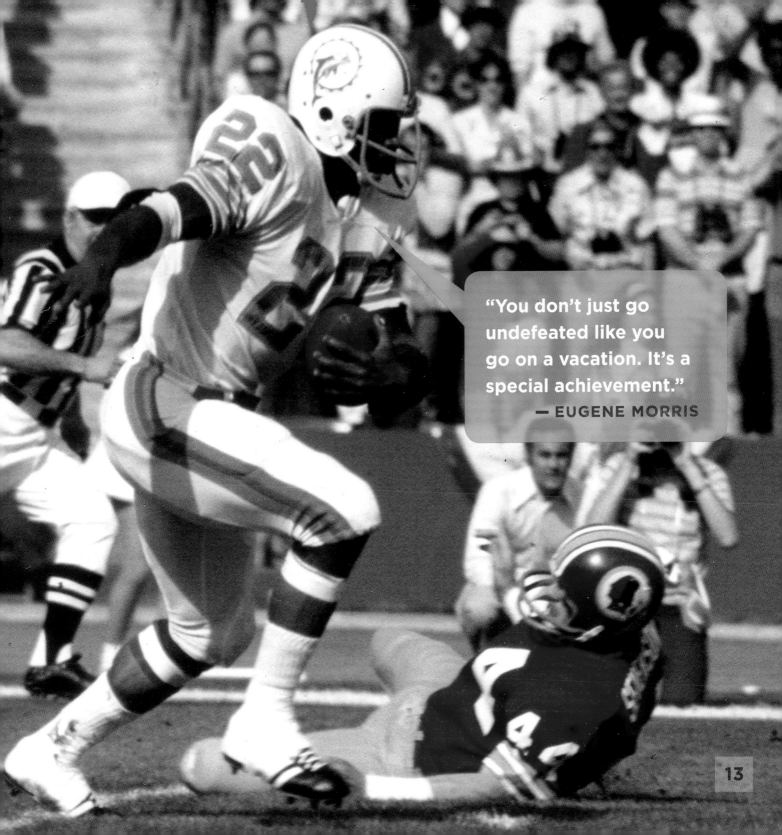

"You don't just go undefeated like you go on a vacation. It's a special achievement."

— EUGENE MORRIS

13

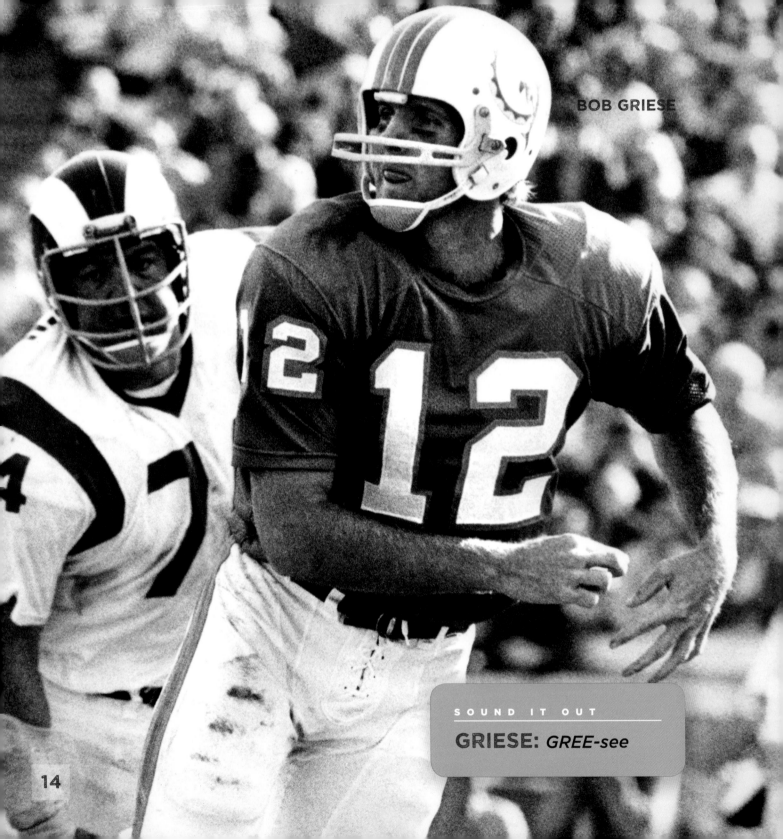

BOB GRIESE

THE DOLPHINS' STORY

The Dolphins started playing in 1966. They were part of the American Football League (AFL) then. The Dolphins did not win much until they hired coach Don Shula in 1970.

Smart quarterback Bob Griese helped make the Dolphins much better, too. They won the Super Bowl after both the 1972 and 1973 seasons!

FAMOUS DOLPHINS

GARO YEPREMIAN
1970–78
Garo was a kicker from a European country called Cyprus. He made many big field goals for Miami.

DAN MARINO

In 1983, the Dolphins got a new quarterback named Dan Marino. He threw 48 touchdown passes in 1984 to help Miami get to the Super Bowl. This time, the Dolphins lost.

MARK CLAYTON / 1983-92

Mark joined Miami in 1983. He was a wide receiver who caught many passes from Dan Marino.

17

ZACH THOMAS

WIDE RECEIVER
BRIAN HARTLINE

Linebacker Zach Thomas helped Miami play great defense in the 1990s. Zach made more than 1,000 tackles in his Dolphins **career**.

In 2007, Miami was a bad team. It won 1 game and lost 15. But Miami bounced back the next season to win 11 games!

By 2013, Miami fans cheered for players like speedy linebacker Cameron Wake. They hoped the Dolphins would soon be a Super Bowl **contender** once again!

CAMERON WAKE

FACTS FILE

CONFERENCE/DIVISION:
American Football
Conference, East Division

TEAM COLORS:
Aqua and orange

HOME STADIUM:
Sun Life Stadium

SUPER BOWL VICTORIES:
VII, January 14, 1973
   14–7 over Washington
   Redskins
VIII, January 13, 1974
   24–7 over Minnesota
   Vikings

NFL WEBSITE FOR KIDS:
http://nflrush.com

RUNNING BACK
RICKY WILLIAMS

GLOSSARY

captain — a player who is a team leader and calls out plays to his teammates

career — all the years that an athlete plays

contender — a talented team that has a good chance of winning a championship

INDEX